orogeny

orogeny

O

Irène Mathieu

WINNER OF THE 2016
BOB KAUFMAN BOOK PRIZE
SELECTED BY MEGAN KAMINSKI

orogeny by Irène Mathieu
Published by Trembling Pillow Press
New Orleans, LA
ISBN-13: 978-0-9964757-6-1
Copyright © 2017 Irène Mathieu

Typesetting and Design: Megan Burns
Cover Image: Irène Mathieu
Cover Design: JS Makkos
Copyedit: Kia Alice Groom

Trembling
Pillow
PRESS

Table of Contents

iii. the clay jar remembers

iv. when did you get so?

orogeny

for my parents

i. speak good dreams into your fist

introduction

Pangaea was the first woman. when the world's water broke it broke over her back and she uncurled and spread into the rocks and gaps that would eventually become us.

being alone so long she had her own language. when a meteor hit somewhere it tickled she had a laugh for that and when the ocean ran up her greening belly she had a word for that feeling which is no longer pronounceable in any human tongue.

because her being contained every thing she had no words for some things like what we call *sickness want love separation* and if you could speak to her today through a Paleozoic interpreter she would not be able to describe them – as if someone asked you how you beat your heart.

when she had children they were born and died right there, in the same round room and she knew everything about how to deliver her babies and gently envelop them again when they ran out.

her body changed as all bodies do. she sighed as the Tethys ocean closed
            opened the Atlantic with a long scream   she was trying
to put a seed into every part that shifted even though she was still
connected below knowing that oceans would bend the horizons and trick
her children into thinking themselves separate tribes.

the greatest problem was the language. there was no way to pass it down and so what the first woman knew we now must feel (and not all of us do) our clumsy tongues trying and failing to explain it.

hydronymy

inside you is
a bayou
a lake where the
ghosts you carry
sit
cypress knees up.

someone said the
Choctaw first called
the bowl of water
in your belly
bayuk,
small stream.

you remember
the roughness of your
mother's fingers as
she made a braided channel
of your hair.

you always had
alligator teeth
the swamp murk
under your tongue
warm and moving
slowly.

you were always
a biter,
had crawfish curled
inside your wrists
to pinch what dipped
its fingers into the water.

you have heron's shins
you flit through fields–

taste salt marsh reeds
straws of sugarcane
free–

your eyes
two blue moons
on either end of a month
holding all of time
inside you holding
all of water.

primum non nocere

first
        the soul must find
a body.

a monarch
                        must fly
into the mouth
                        of a fetus.
a mother must lay
            on her side

dreaming good dreams
stories
            that have no name.

the opposite of love
            is power.
a mother

must be prepared
to be powerless
and terrified
            at all times

any mothering soul
a hibiscus
            inverting
by opening

            offering nectar
to any passing
            hummingbird.

the Blue-throated Mountaingem
has a heart that can beat

        1,260 times
per minute.

it has a window of sky
painted on its neck.

you are both
        a small frenetic
body
tattooed with heaven
and a mother

        a whole ecosystem
mirrored behind your eyes.

hover
        leave vortices in
your wake
then welcome
        yourself

smooth the air
and speak good dreams
into your fist.

ii. church of the frontera (the empire machine does not have a lover)

epidemiology

                when you were not looking
the wasted world made a hole and
                that was how it got inside you.
in you it began to store assaults, genocide,
                and even petty grievances.
the hole was widened as you slept by
                the claws of dreams
slow ripping and sometimes by a
                snaggletooth saw that woke you up
gasping and sweaty
                you did what you could to fill that
time capsule – your mouth
                but the world followed you
down unlit blocks and it was there
                on your shoulder
a shadow-colored rat gnawing
                in the shadow of your scapula
strips of muscle, cracks of bone
                so when you have questions
(why? why me? why now?)
                it isn't that the making of love,
even food, prayer,
                did not smooth something.
the world will always tear us open
make its home in our blood   *its scudding muzzle*
                its hijack of arteries.

the benediction of Our Lady of Hyperglycemia

there are a lot of things they
don't teach you in Catholic school.

for instance, is there such a thing
as overdosing on prayer?

does martyrdom become a health hazard
at any point before knives are involved?

how can we feel the quiet current
of Too Much in our capillaries

and root it out before fossilizing
in sugar silt?

if we clabber our blood will we
be considered for beatification?

and isn't the fork a way
to worship, too?

my grandpa is a down South
Catholic. on Christmas, he said,

they used to drink and box.
he said they used to ride into the fields

and suck juice from sugarcane
were always full of gumbo,

pecan pies, pound cake, hog's head cheese
blood sausage, red beans and rice, half-shell oysters

wouldn't dream of spilling a sweet sauce drop.
this is the way it was done in New Orleans,

the most Catholic city north of the Gulf.
when you die, thick-blooded,

you will die full of tastes and walk through
the door to the Holy Trinity simmering in pork fat.

there are things you could eat
or sacrifice, and someone would name

you a saint on account of either one.

what's your name

heavy chimes
clot the hours
in the air and

my blood asks, *do bones
carry future memories
in their marrows?*

waiting for a face
that is a mirror, I
turn the page of

a tome that lists
only my name
my name my name.

tonight each cicada sings
its name, the only
one it knows,

and when I stepped out
the door this morning
and a chipmunk

slammed into my shoe, it
couldn't remember
its name for a moment.

our eyes met – I blurted
sorry, sweetie! its name
I did not know

an emptiness arching
around my tongue
as if to know and say it

could undo our small
collision.

although winter in Chile, it was summer on Mars[1]

and winter in Chile is summer in Chicago,
is rainy season in Cambodia, is dry season
in Cusco, is a wet or dry or fattening or dying season for someone
everywhere.

at some point there is an egg and a chicken emerges; at some point the
chicken and another chicken beget more cracking eggs and chickens
feathering over fenced yards of mud or clawing at the dirt that cakes
the throat of a farm girl forever traipsing from fence to barn to kitchen
door to fence... or is she an Argentine girl who isn't really a girl, but a
bereaved mother circling a square older than her grandfather, shouting
her throat raw *what have you done with my child?!* or is she a Gazan girl
pulling up rubble to dig for books or bones that have exploded into ash,
or bones, ducking from bombs, pulling rubble, books, ducking?

whatever proper nouns we put in front of a person tell us the exact curve
of the circle of hell that loops her or him, them, etc.

or is she me? breathlessly watching the sun swallow a mountain and
believing everything, then washing up on a craggy shore covered in salt
wounds, believing nothing, then watching the bleeding sun in wonder,
then bleeding onto a beach

or is she you?

it doesn't matter much whether you claim Mars or Earth as home; if you
spin you always come around again or everything comes around to you,
dirt or grief or bombs or waves around again and around and again every
winter of bombs raining into the next summer of dirt again around and
again

how can you write a new thing
                    in a universe composed of circles

the Black American gets her travel fellowship and goes abroad

I. an exercise:

the positionality of placeholders

there is something that wants to be said
there is something that wants to be said
there is something that wants to be said

there is something
that wants the dark birth
of words.

she is on a line
the passport holds her up
little blue woven book
little blue book
little blue
little
she

the empire machine is dreaming. the empire machine rolls over. the empire machine wakes up. the empire machine stretches. the empire machine does not have a lover. the empire machine makes coffee. the empire machine goes to work.

II.
I promise you,
that girl she looked
just like my sister
cousin daughter
niece comadre
you know —
la morena
who lives next
to the colmado
that always smells

of raw meat and
plátanos.

III. what she says:

one day I dream myself
on the outside of a flying plane.
I grip a rope twisted through
a loop on the wing, and the
wind scoops everything
out of my mouth.

inside my bones an unborn
old woman is stretching and dancing.
my skin feels too tight.

I return
swallowing Spanish.
Border Control squints
interrogates
x-rays
finally says
welcome home.

I am overflowing
and the taxi driver sees.
ah, you miss your country?
his eyes are soft.
I cannot speak.

(and regarding a bra Made In _____)
I wonder what woman with
a transatlantic face like mine

has worked calluses into her
fingers for the comfort of

nude-colored breasts. nude
being khaki, as in fatigues
or nude being cream, as in
of the crop.

try wearing:
a river
barbed wire
gold
black
dried blood
a harvest
lost languages
a seam
I mean a border
and how will you find
your way home?
and how will you find?
and how?
will you find?
and you how?
how will you?
how you?
how you.
home will find
you and how.

Breve descripción de la noble ciudad de Santiago de los Caballeros de Guatemala y puntual noticia de su lamentable ruina ocasionada de un violento terremoto el día 29 de julio de 1773[2]

we have come back and stand again
in this place, wondering how time
managed to fold on itself and curl up.

there are frozen smells around us
like smoke drifts – the nixtamal,
her hair, the beaten sheets baking
next to the lime tree in the sun.

we would like to write about this place
but the unutterable sadness would
burst our ledgers into flames.

we would like to be the dirt here
because it is an undying eye,
it is a mirror of the sun, it is the one
promise of being we did not know
we had tucked under our scalps
the day before the earth
took us home, and the dogs,
and the children, and all the little
heartbreaks we thought of as
our names.

Pangaea explains the earthquake

I had to shake
to see if I was still
alive.

and I split.
and the crevasse
was a wound.
and a sound.

see you, or parts of you,
falling in?
see exposed femurs and
orphaned feet?

see where buildings buckled,
bit through themselves?
see who did and didn't
scream?

I found that I
was alive.
but you were half-dead,
you masters of slow
suicide,
you armored beasts
swathed in denial
roped around your wrists –
see how you throw yourselves
into the ocean and claim
to have ten lives?

observation in a small country

a braided girl bounces into
a corner store that smells like garbage.
salsa gushes in the sunlight
plays under her heels
and the radio announcer asks
are you a sex addict?
sex addiction is a serious disease.

things are close together here –
trauma and innocence
are neighbors –
dances and bullets
share afternoon coffee –
a virgin beach once
slept with a gold mine.

the salsa flares and
flies land on green bananas.
when what ripens splits to rot
the memory of sunlight will be
excruciating.

Nuestra Señora de Tennessee supplicates Coatlalopeuh

La Virgen de Guadalupe's Indian name is *Coatlalopeuh*. *Coatlalopeuh* is descended from, or is an aspect of, earlier Mesoamerican fertility and Earth goddesses. The earliest is *Coatlicue*. [...] Before the change to male dominance, *Coatlicue*, the Lady of the Serpent Skirt, contained and balanced dualities of male and female, light and dark, life and death.

         - from *Borderlands/La Frontera: The New Mestiza*, by Gloria Anzaldúa

the sun dusts to dust-colored
every rustling thing
and every unmoving metal scrap
on the frontera which is nowhere
near a border.
the dust-colored grass wrangles
up through asphalt
the dust-colored billboards:
your ad here. call Tiffani.
advertise here.
the dust-colored pockmarks
on her teeth
supermercado y carnicería
discount tobacco
latino america auto sales
church of the
church of the
church of the
pebble-biting grit-fisted niñas
with ponytails like switches
church of the
quick-eyed boys
sullen-eyed boys
eyes behind bent blinds
hands covered in dust
church of the
hands covered in dust.
discount tobacco
video city

police SUVs shiny as toys
beside a scab-colored pick-up
church of the
advance cash title loans.
ten in a dust-colored trailer.
down the road is
miracle baptist church
but church of the
frontera is dusted over
with peeling sideboards
with a very small cockroach
you almost don't notice.
the eight children drunk off sugar
pretending this isn't
the edge of the world
like they don't toe a frontera
and have dust-colored dreams.

the weight and dimensions of my prayers

prayers of lead
prayers of limestone and pages for

women's bodies piled on the side of the freeway, no one rubbernecking.
women's bodies filling art museums, blocking the paintings.
women's bodies packing school buses, a whole yellow swarm.
women's bodies lying in every pew of every cathedral in France

no one singing hymns of their hair, psalms of their palms
their multicolored skins painted in stained glass patches.
every wreck of a shadowed sister thumbs me deeper
into a pile of dust.

what is a woman's body?
it cannot fit into any room:
the thousand sparks in my feet.
shipwrecks. kisses. whiskey.
soldered melodies. soldiered acquiescences.
brimming frivolities of vital importance.
turns at every turn. paper and strings. stone.

the first time I found salvation it was
in a library, on my knees bent before the spines
of books. before I knew the weight and dimensions
of my prayers I imagined them as nebulous supernovae
trembling toward gravities.

this is without having seen the
women's bodies, feet to heads, lining dead cotton fields.
women's bodies filling the cellars of every New England home built
        before 1950.
women's bodies in the parking lots of fast food restaurants.
women's bodies in the basement warehouses of office buildings.
women's bodies carpeting the floor of the Atlantic, undulating softly
        forever.

I broke a thumb and a pinky finger once.
they were splinted and fretted over, so that I never

guessed my body could be broken and tossed onto a pile
of women's bodies that no one recognized. so when I

recognized kneecaps and collarbones I began to pray,
asking the center of the Earth to put our pieces back together.

women's bodies choking up the space under bridges.
women's bodies packed vertically in vacant lots.
women's bodies folded efficiently into plywood crates.
women's bodies curled around cacti, all dried sockets and dust clothing.
women's bodies sleeping their un-sleep in the beds of eighteen-wheelers.
women's bodies clogging construction sites, bones lined along naked
          beams.
women's bodies tangled in mountains of dirt and abandoned machetes.

when you rise from peaceful storied oblivion and
realize your spine can be hunted and broken and no one
really needs the under-floorboard or trash bag or ditch
that will contain your woman's body, you become unspeakably
sad. you might start preemptively disintegrating.

you had better have a story sewn into the lining of your jacket
when they come for your body. and if that doesn't save you,
you had better have another body, preferably not a woman's.

Pangaea knows exactly what I mean

I want to be taken care of
      he says   shy and simple
he says   I want you to take care of me
he spells the exact shape of the wound
and puts my thumbs in it
            his latest mouth

the mothers have mothered so long
the daughters are born chanting it
in their sleep
      sleep-walking it in their day
laughing it in their moons:
daughtering is nothing but
learning to mother.
but who mothers the mothers?

who mothers the mothers is
an invisible flying elk
a helium-filled apparition:
      yes, a party trick.

who mothers the mothers
      is a math riddle:
it is the same distance a train
travels in the time it takes
for a 3-gram hummingbird
to collect nectar from fifty foxgloves
if the foxgloves are the color of
myocardium and the train leaves
from a latitude of
[your birth year] N, [the current year] W
keeping in mind that foxglove extract
can be a heart-stopping elixir
particularly in women.

I want to be taken care of
but I don't know how to tell
anyone else to do what I have done

for centuries without knowing
it was the work for all our
soft shoulders.

I tell him
you had better learn to size up
a wound   the opening
of a train's fuel tank
                    you had better
learn to pour nectar in
slow and gentle as your
grandmother once did.

belonging here

the brain and body are
subject to all types of flash flooding –

                          in the brain and body
                I am
                a wreck of states
          a solid/liquid Arkannesota
                    Virginifornia

all types of gaseous bodies can fit inside

my own – call them ghosts
or digested artifacts from

          the great Crock-Pot of Cracker Barrel's
          Midwestern fantasy Thanksgiving special,
a video game so sublime

                    that it ends somewhere down the Mississippi
                    amidst fried chicken, chewed-up baseballs.

                        in the swamp
              houses on stilts lean on each other
                  with nothing but my tibias   and wet rot
                  to prop them up.

        my skin, these United
floors of cold copper,

                    feels electric and probably is
              wired through tight as a light switch.

before your eyes I metamorphosed
        again and again –
now bear,
now four-leafed clover,
now trailer park,

and you.

            you held me
as one would a tender flame,

directly
            in a hand made
of cloth.

Pangaea bets on a racehorse

this one moves clean as a whistle
through a cut field, the grass low
and sharp, the earth packed and ready –
my skin freshly shaved and taut.

see his clever flank studded with
constellations? the river in his tail,
the smart clop of hooves the
response to my call in his bones.

the weakest part of his body is the
eye, a tiny globe of tragedy and
ash, the shambled house of his
name's memories – the rot of the race.

every millennium I sigh with regret –
oh, consciousness, a luscious devil,
you fog around the sweet, sweet apple
studded with worm, let my horses go,

let them forget everything they ever
won.

g as in god

for Ahmed Al-Jumaili

the woman announced

    "please proceed to gate g, as in god."

g as in 99 divided by 11
then re-imagined
as in the buildings de-imagined,
turned upside down
and shaken out one September,
which we call the same as
the American flag
    which we call freedom
    which is the number we call
    when we want god
to appear as an ambulance

which is the number that was called
    21 days after Ahmed Al-Jumaili
    boarded a plane through gate g
    (fingers stretched toward
    that same promise)
because his blood was coloring
a blooming peony on the snow
(a pomegranate shot through,
exploding house of jewel)
red as a wet 9, red as a siren
red as stripes on a flag, red as hell.

after I read about the death
of Ahmed Al-Jumaili
I dreamt of a gate and plane

a man and his wife walking toward it
with every dream balled up in their fists
and their shoes filling with blood.

bones

the bones' heft
the same weight as paper
a ream
same confetti when
shredded
same ache of words
sliced into half-
letters and syl
lables dismemb
ered.

we have misremembered.
every time we
(accidentally)   open
up the earth
pressed tight as a
stubborn mouth
the erased stories
float to the surface
the bones reassemble
into abcs.

consider the stretch
of the lips when saying
hvala or *gracias*.
see how gratitude keeps
the two sides close.
our continents look
like bodies with lips
drawn in strange
directions.
when the lips say words
such as *war* and *border*
the land implodes
people fall into those
        sinkholes.

does all pain cycle back
to prod until we perform
the proper rites?

it's as if we were
an addled child
taking loose teeth
and burying them
into the fleshy pads
of our feet
after years
forgetting why each step
still bleeds.

making strangers

I remember standing among
the ruins in Tarragona, thinking
how through holes in the wall
the sea sat wide as a mouth.
raising my camera, what could
be tossed into that shout?

on the train back to Barcelona
I called upon forgetting,
something in a frieze
a thing frozen. the Egyptians
across the sea buried their
dead with honey, the only
sweet thing that won't decay.

in Italian tombs even wine
has gone vinegar, not a
suggested libation for your
average catacomber.
I would like to leave
something in this crypt –
the common air that passed
from one to another's lungs

sealed in six stone slabs
then funneled into the earth
below the sigh of
shifting prayers. I'd like
to think that one day an
earthquake will open under
the cathedral long after
the last human dies

will swallow what I buried
and digest it at the center –

the final evidence turning back
into salt and ash, as if
you and I had never met.

love poem at the end of empire

UVA student Martese Johnson bloodied during arrest by ABC agents
Daily Progress headline, March 18, 2015

because a boy had been beaten
the night before,
bloodied

by uniformed men
patrolling the plantation,
I mean campus,

and because you have cousins at universities,
and they look like that boy smiling,
before,

and because we are slaves,
I mean brown, we are simply brown
and in the wrong country,

or because our country is wrong,
you got turned inside out,
drenched in your terror,

and I with empty hands
could not dry you.
at night

I turn my phone on silent,
always. but still,
my body knew to wake and reach

for it when you called me,
early, to say

I love you.
the end of everything
being in its beginning,

I should mention that when
foreign men wrongly made
this country, they thought, *kill,*

and when I first met you
on a campus browning with autumn,
I thought, *home.*

because of this,
even in silence I could pull you
up from a dream of blood,

and you could pull me out of sleep
with a silent ring, because
what could be more home

in this sort of country?

our boy

for Jordan Davis, Renisha McBride, Trayvon Martin, Aiyana Stanley-Jones, Tamir Rice, Michael Brown, etc.

it's two years now
our boy's been gone.
two years since
the brightness closed.

our boy was bright!
if you could have seen him
he would have burned
straight through your
retinas into your brain,
passed down the blood
vessels in your neck
into your heart.

you couldn't help
smiling at our boy.
they said those blood
vessels are what

the bullet blew out
lead dynamite going off
in the dark tunnel that
carried life all
through his body.
no train could pass
through the wreckage
the system amok.

they say first your heart
beats faster and then your
breath picks up, trying to
make the difference
but nothing undoes a
mountain quicker than

an explosion. you can
go down the hill behind
our house, where our boy
used to play, and cross the
muddy creek, and fight
the brambles until the woods
give way to an open field.
beyond it you'll see the
bald skulls of mountains.
some men find nothing sacred

not even their Mother.
some will kill because it's
their inheritance. our boy
was bright! brighter than
anything could be pulled
from a mine. our boy *was*
the mountain. it's been
years since anything sacred

was respected. blasting
through that child's vessels
must have been nothing,
but then, you know nothing

of how we made them –
putting our love into a big
mixing bowl and stepping
aside so the Earth could
work through us – the most
sacred work we ever did.
the brightness burst out
of us and we thought *this*

was finally a light that
would never turn off,
even though we went

to bed every night with
prayers between our teeth.

if you could have seen
our boy, I swear, it might
have put the pieces back
in place. it might have
closed the circle. we might
have been safe all together.

Pangaea carries one of her sons home

when that boy's body fell
into my arms he felt heavy
as a century
his mouth was open
his chest was bloom.

to see a son murder a son
and his cold child's body
buckle under the steel
wrenched from my own
dark hallways is no way

to live the end of your days.
my hair on fire
my blood laced
my hands blown and broken

my son balled and crumpled,
a bit of paper
a shred of a boy
a secret written down
and sent back up.

estrangement

human is a kind of confusion.
the ways we've gone astray are

the centipede's terrified march
from under my bed

    how a cockroach can pull
    a scream from the core of my mother
    that shakes all our blood

        the easy stomp that splays
        a spider under some dumb heel.

who fears?

    then there's the chicken's
    small-eyed terror

        the cow quartered and slung
        into plastic package

        the exotic alligator skinned
        and stretched over someone's
        socked, stewing toes.

what is foreign here?

        there are greenbacks packed
        in elephant tusk

        and manatees tattooed with
        missing pieces

        and for pieces of the big game
        poachers pull the big guns,
        pop-pop on pampas.

who can see and hear?

they must watch us – two-leggeds
covered in cotton, appetites crashing
through forests and plains – and
wonder who lost us, what force
made us un-animal.

if all you can think of are the rhinos

Shim E. "One of Africa's Most Treasured Species Could Be Completely Wiped Out by 2020."

- PolicyMic.com 2014

after reading where a man
from a Foundation said that
>there will probably be no free-living rhinos
>as the remaining numbers will be fenced off
>in military-style compounds which are
>alarmed and heavily guarded by armed patrols

and you write to the last rhinos before they
go extinct in a jail run by a Foundation to save
them you will feel a few kinds of sad:

you in a place that long stopped loving
you, breathing its air still. someone's
rainy season. someone's forest fire.
>a baby rhino is called
>a calf, as in, *there's a pain in my.*
someone's lost calf, dancing away forever.

the rhinos' cut trunks in
the picture look like conical trees laid down
to die. rotted-log innards. the heroes are
the park rangers reportedly gunned down
by blood ivory gangs. the article says

the British are sending help, which
is a few kinds of sad, such as every
water-colored thought running down
your arms and also inertia. an object in
motion.

the water balloon clouds want to
suffocate us. the homicidal sky.
did you hear the theory about
global warming? the Earth's fever.
she's better off without us.
no such thing as an outside force.

the political is personal

something inside of me gets deader and deader
as the dying things collect, limb over limb, foot
touching face. something gets steel-er with every
cold eye, something sharpens and sharpens in the
lengthening silence, something does not let me
live. something is a panicked rabbit smelling
gunpowder and blood, something is a limping deer
feeling itself turn from ancestral finger of forest
to hunted, something is forgetting its name. there's
no remedy of touch or song that sticks.
something's been consumed, burned up, charred
down, made ashen and blunted. something no
longer believes.

> something else knows all this is happening
> and mourns, shut up in the bathroom,
> hunched over the radiator, shriveled as a
> let-go balloon.

something knows it will rise again, but it has no
idea when and can't wait forever

Pangaea's 16 questions

what on earth
is a planet.
good goddess & good gracious & spacious
presumptuous to plan it.
what on earth
have you planted.
what harvest. what handed royalty wielded
the spade until red clay yielded
drops of blood & later magic buttered fingers
& crosses.
& dams.
what grown-green sound of fury clanged.
what galloped. what ranged.
which dim echoes did you heed. (none.)
which ghosts can sleep soundly.
which ghosts take nightly Ambien.
which ghosts have given in
to the infinity of a scream.
anything halved and halved again
and so on will never disappear
just dilute and scatter.
why are you surprised
to smell it on the wind still.
gravity holds things close
the atmosphere a smothering embrace.
why are you self-righteous.
why do you look down.
where is a planet.
where can it go
but inside itself.
the natural history of a pirouette
in outer space is condensation.

the Orishas spend a day as humans

Elegguá was a grease-streaked boy
begging change at intersections.

Ogún was a cane-cutter missing two fingers,
sweet machete sap turning him bitter.

Yemayá was a community health worker who
was teaching new mothers to breastfeed.

Olokun was the hungry fisherman who stepped
from his hut to a silver sunrise of dead shad.

Babalú Ayé used to drive trucks bursting with plátanos;
he coughs in the campo waiting for PEPFAR.

Taiwó and Kehinde have bellies stretched like
drums full of worms and giggles.

Oyá sat cross-legged with a hundred other women
on a mountain road the gold miners wanted to pass.

Changó leaned over colmado counters
gave mujeres free gum in exchange for a dance.

Obba's scarf covered half her missing ear and the other
worked twice as well to sell sun-warm avocados.

the day passed. no one recognized them.
our countries spend every day filled with gods

but every day the labyrinth grows more
concentric circles, the burning tire flames

leaping higher.

love poem in the time of climate change

Dear One,
you are much lighter than a comet
and made of the same things
and this frightens me.

what impossible sky could
hold you? not my arms –
too small, too breakable.

Philadelphia, December 2015:
seventy degrees and balmy.
the rock has never been
this hot, this close to explosion,
and yet we talk of children
stubbornly as humans.

where will they live when
the water is gone? drink me
for eternity and I would not
be enough water for us both.
this is a simple equation.

I sit beside the window
watching the hot rain
melt the breakable rock

and remember us running
past the river, licking our
fingers covered in cinnamon,
thoughtless as air, no idea of
the river's heaviness beside us.
where do we live, with the
water rising heavy all around?

I have a vision I'm an
early salamander, unsure
of the cue to enter, eyes wild
and confused, rolled under

the rubber heel of a car,
my family not yet born.

I travel back through time
to meet you (remember?).

where will we love?
        the window asks,
and in response I describe your face.

iii. the clay jar remembers

Pangaea's aubade

having been called, I woke up
in the great gravitational womb
and loved every force.

how do you replace that?
the original sin was not what
you think. it was thinking
the forces separate.

here I am, getting carried away,
as if I can clearly remember those
days. so much stardust has come
between us since then, and what
memory is not mostly myth?

if you want to know, I would
not undo any motion. my birth
is a dead little morning
memory blankets and smothers.

other fires have since been lit
and burned down to skull.
I reminisce so you know
the story of our blood, so that
you will have something to
sing when you wake up.

glossopteris

we have seen the millennia-long
purple net of rain
we have seen it dye the earth into
deep ice
and we have watched the robot
dinosaurs creak and rupture
at midnight.
we have seen without an eye.

we have seen the bubble and stink
of your animal skin
rise garish as a sun released from
a silent cave
we have seen aliens land to strew
their secrets,
viruses that slip into the strings
of things and twist, hard.

yes, we remember contact,
and the day the sky cracked
and each time the ocean vomited.
we reveled in the outstretched
fronds of existence
that you now feel only at the moment
before death.

we felt the deep gulp of extinction
and did not weep.

what is an eye?
what is a body?
it contains us but is not us.
inert and glossy, we are the
opposite of tongues in stone,

the stamp of breath
the long rain's progeny
the green and invisible o.

Day No. 1

first snow. the year is 17 days old.
on the day before the day before

Christmas, fat earthworms slithered
onto the sidewalk to drown next to
limp cigarettes. it was warm as

breath, hot and moist as a question
out loud. here is the sky,
crying mightily, turning to gold.

I haven't learned the way home yet,
except that it will be through a page.

think back to your first teacher,
your mother's blood, like gentle
hands pushing your body into its

shape (Universal Truth No. 1).
our mind might as well be made
of brick walls, the way the world

is filled with echoes. dance
or weep first, but I guarantee

you'll be doing both. first
17. only way home is through.
only good cigarette is a dead one.

honor the earthworm, its echo
chamber of blood, small sacrifices
dying for Christ on the concrete.

compassion

for the way a deer
would turn tail in the
dusty dim, no warning.
for the dimming.
for the briny lover's way of
holding my skin
with his beard. the dredge,
        its debris.

I learned the illusion
of tidiness
from the rows of desks and
godforsaken cubbies –
a mirage that still has me
knee-deep in detritus,
slogging toward land that
erodes before my eyes.

a man has promised to meet me there.
get ready for nothing:
the way a dream bolts,
skittish   unfriendly
        the way the oasis muddies,
the waking.

I try to conjure
the fleeing deer's shape
        years later
in the therapist's armchair
her clinician's smile
made of nickel.
grains of sweat
in my hair
the summer wind
stuck in my throat.

what looked like land
could have been a

barnacled spit of flotsam.
what seemed a deer
could easily have been
a stray mutt rooting
through the neighbor's trash.

strays

they move as one body
of many dogs – a pack
of gods, the jaws in a school
of fur-covered pirañas,
the scrapers, the chain-link fence
scramblers, the howling mavericks,
all trash-ravaging limbs and tails,
guardians of fish skeletons
and stale bread, guardians and
thieves of life, scrawny gatekeepers,
the rat bouncers of the gutters' maw,
landfill fashionistas, with photographic
memories the witnesses of our
full scale of tragedies, sentinels of
the canine gene pool, sharp-toothed
musicians of a growly blues, the percussion
in the symphony of the city,
the staccato undressing of shy
morning, the dull-pawed dancers.

the dogs are the architects of the street,
the wardens, the patron saints.
step aside for them, they gather the dirt
and feed the fleas, and wrangle life
after life from their heavy wombs –

human,

the dogs are midwives and scholars, too.

the pharmacy of noises

old friends, lovers, dead dreams,
flocks of crows, brush fires,
& endangered species:

I am writing you all down.
I am writing the way you sound.
I am cataloguing your voices
in a pharmacy of noises:

desperate cawing at sunset
for the days I am a leafless tree.

the final sigh of words as they
swam down your cheek.

the surprising roar a mountain makes
when being shaved by flames.

how cold a comet is.
how breathless is a hurricane.

just think of the lands
devastated by men
who wanted to catch all the sounds
screw them up into glass vials.

and even you, you wanted to
lasso the rain. you wanted to
weave the doorslam into your hair
and wear bangles that clanked
with your grandmother's cough
that winter she lay dying
long before any of you knew it.

no one here is innocent and
no one's evolved out of illness.

in this land we suffer silences
deep as the white-hot heart
of earth, and as blazing.

how small this continent is
if you think about it.
how mundane are all our deaths.

in the pharmacy of noises
you collect a tiny packet of
powdered sounds.
you go home.
you mix it with a glass of
warm milk. you sleep
like a baby.

languages

you say, *a spray of starlings.*
I say, *the pre-pre-eventide.*

you touch my wrist.
I say, *excruciation.*

you say, *here, in this sky.*
I say, *here, in this sentence.*

you say, *earth.*
I point to the ocean.

I bark. you blink.
I barter. you sing.

you have the eyes of an owl.
I have the eyes of a deer.

you sit like an ancient rock,
some deep carbon ore.

I curl around myself
like an animal without bones.

I am possessed by the tides.
you follow a closer gravity.

at times we land on the same
wave and it sounds like spring.

you say, *what do you want, dear?*
I say, *everything inside the moon.*

theory of multiple theories

I've written multiple theories about love.

I've watched a robin hop desperately around its mate splayed like a
broken fan.
I've seen cancer swell under a baby girl's jaw, and I've seen her parents.
I've refused goodbyes and have swallowed whole sentences that snagged
in my gut, rotted, soaked into my belly until it burned.

misunderstood or perfectly understood I never could say for sure, but I've
been called a rare bird by a boy and
I've seen myself in dreams as a Quetzalcoatl crashing to earth and
wondered,
do I have feathers or do I breathe fire?

in the mirror I am supreme witch-goddess of the in-between world
where each of us
places the fetal dream of ourselves, a sea of curled and floating ideas
filled with un-words.
in the eyes of the sky I am a drop of sweat.
in the mirror of the past I am a wandering frog, uncommitted to the river
or the bank.
            years from now I will learn silence.

I've drowned stars in a glass of rum
shoved sand under the nail of my thumb
sucked a cigar until it knotted my
stomach into rubber.
it's what we place between ourselves and everything else that burrows in,
bruises.

in the eyes of the earth I am a jar on a pottery wheel, spinning glistening
clay guesswork of supreme hands.
I smell like underground.
            years from now I will be filled with water.

soil

the way you say *soil* sounds
like *soul,* as in

after we walked through the woods
my feet were covered in soul

when it rains
the soul turns to mud

the soul is made of decomposed
plant and animal matter;

edaphology is the study of the soul's
influence on living things

while pedology is the study of how
soul is formed, its particular granularity.

you are rooted in a certain red patch
of soul that bled you and your

hundred cousins to life, a slow
warm river you call home.

maybe there is soul under everything,
even when we strike rock first.

the way you say *soil* you make
a poem out of every speck of dirt.

shadow talk

a deer in the hand is worth two in the sky
my shadow says to you
as the moon jumps between worlds,
from waist to waist.

you invite the ghosts in from the fields
they come carrying their bowls
I pray on my haunches

wax on a table is worth two on a candle
says a ghost.
I pour, pour, pour, my chin tilted—

every time we drive past the old house
our heads turn like pitchers—
I hear the bullfrogs deep in my throat
I smell the moonshine under our feet—
the sacred way grass remembers

you've never been abandoned in a dream
I aim to keep the fishing line between
this world and the other
clear and strong as rain—

so you can change shapes but you
can never disappear.

pieces

the piece of your mother
that broke off
and later was given your name
does not remember
the way her body rearranged
channels of blood
to your growing self.

think of how I felt,
Atlantica cracking off
Gondwana, rivers left
to pour into the
widening sea
like tongues
talking to no one.

the truth will come back
to you in pieces:

years of silence
then one day
the lover's warm breath
in a moment so filled with light
it made you cry for years after.

the truth in bubbles
you released bursting up
from the bottom of a lake
where you were swimming
toward the sun.

the truth on the first day of fall
water stripped from the air
so the light is
uncompromising
bending around nothing.

a thing is named for what
it is not.
think of how I felt, nameless.

you cannot imagine
the ache that wholeness,
rent, left.
you write
     I am this
you erase
     not that

your life a search
for the space from which
you came.

the law of conservation of love

the sheets of rain that passed over me
five minutes apart
on a tropical beach once:

the same sudden submersion
understanding is when it
ambushes me
the same brightening sun
between each water-curtain

the growing knowledge
that no raindrop will ever
leave this world.

the rim

around the most delicate orbit of me   you circle, a moon mining
sugar
                 trawling for my sweet collapse,
         planetary wink and ruin,
      thousand monsoons.

my under-thighs a roof blown
to wooden matchsticks in a storm
             you move to the glint of detritus,
                rough-edged crater for birthing
                   emptied husks.

      there is a small bird in my throat
      that will not stop echoing the sound
      of water rolling off her feathers,
            and under a trembling leaf you find
            a tree frog, its pulse so insistent
            you think I have grown a second heart.

             you're a scavenger, rooting for rot
            under fallen branches. I'm at my
            dimmest and dampest, earthy, pliable,
            nothing more alive than hair and the
         movement of skin over bone
kneading water from nothing.

            this is how life began:
               nothing
                 rock
                   water
                     skin.
      take
            a handful of my hair, turn my head
              so I can see the sky opening beyond
                 this one.

if I ever get over the bodies of men

after Rodney Jones

I remember you like this:
what I once felt on top
of a mountain in the Andes,
song-tired and emptied,
when someone spun the fog

back into the sky and I saw a
valley that held everything.
my breath burst the way
it always did when, in bed,
I'd turn over to find myself
between your cedar arms.

yes, this was alive:
sky drawing my body
into singing, like your
arms smooth and bright
as a mirror.

**

we have taken many flights together
and in each time zone I wanted
to put your voice in a locket
around my neck, a music box
of you at every longitude.
I wanted to burn my hand in the
magma under your rib cage
rising and falling as you dreamt.
I wanted a scar on my palm shiny
as a mirror.

**

a man's body is mostly horizon and ocean,
forests springing up on his back

waterfalls on his chest
oil between his thighs.

if I ever get over the bodies of men
I will build a house
on the side of a mountain
and wake up every morning
to trees' embrace. if I get over
I will not buy another plane ticket
or look for messages in translated
newspapers or write another poem.
if I get over I will remember you
like this:

I am the sky and what it
lights up   gives light to:
a birth in every second.
there is nothing more
to remember,
you mirror,
you sky.

harvest

the drying grasses
are a set of strings. my

grandparents are old;
all they do these days
is sing.

when I am old I will
move like a woman
without a mask

in which a season is
nothing but a breath

if a breath is a universe.
be luminescent with me,

I am asking you to move
the way a meadow does, steady

until we reach the sun
on the other side of the earth.

when I am young I will
listen like a sky. I wish

to remember the beauty
of every vegetable –

the blood-filled beet
the delicate squash
how we fed each other
weeping berries.

I am asking you to
fill ourselves up with light
the way plants do, honorably.

no one can fly without it.

when we laid by the river
when we laid by the river
when we laid by the river

we were water.

when I am young
I will fly like a listening sky.

we have been fed.
our bodies glow.
we are sung.

15 signs that you have landed

1. in autumn the air is clearest
the water has been stripped from it
the light bends around nothing.

2. you find yourself plagiarizing yourself.
you knew. you knew.

3. between the gum and the razor blades.
you find it. you keep it. all pennies
look burnt. the customer before you
rushing to placate her toddler with
a Butterfinger. her buttery fingers.
your gem.

4. see how long you can sit in a forest
without noticing any of the trees.

5. unlost and split open
the pomegranate that almost got away
you are ruby seeds everywhere.

6. this winter will be the coldest yet
but every winter after will be warmer
and hotter and hotter and hotter.
you will strip everything off in a storm
of sweat.

7. look at the time! my god.

8. ten jams in a row.
traffic jams. raspberry jams.
finger jams. jammy wines of
ten grapes in a row, you are
floating above vineyards now.
you dance involuntarily to
every jam.

9. but not if you are the sheep
and the shepherd. behind the ditch
in the crush of wool begging, bleating
nothing at the gate.

10. if you are building a time travel
machine and every breath is a small
experiment proving you right.

11. sweet canned tomatoes
your mother is pressure-cooking
and she nods over the great moon
of a pot and shows you where
the seals are so tight they won't leak
or bust open until it's time.

12. you have not grown old
you are not afraid
you don't think about moments
like scrolls. you are
unafraid and unrolled.

13. the question answers itself
in a mirror.

14. the mirror answers herself
in a palm, on a belly, under
a pillow.

15. ah! the clay jar remembers
the mountain from which it
was sculpted.

thermodynamics

my mother first wrangled my hair into a fist of nettles
with the blow dryer, every strand hissing anger.
in school photos I was covered by a cumulus canopy –
haloed child of quickening oak boughs, of holy magnolia
spreading, blossoms first, in a righteous dark tangle.

once I was taken to have my hair texturized –
ambivalent, I watched the white chemicals
smoothed over my head, the foil and the heat,
like soldering a robot's fulgent helmet.
the lye didn't take. on the way home,

I saw train tracks overgrown by sweet ramps and
          little purple flowers   insistent wisteria winding
through the iron ties   coils of ivy splitting   rotted wood
          and I could already feel my hair rejecting the
suggestion of straightness.   secretly, I was proud.

          nothing wild can be turned rigid for long –
the twist and drench of a simple thunderstorm undoes
it all.   the chattering curls burst out with the first wash

        and I emerged from the shower with my head singing,

                  knowing I held the entropy of a forest in my scalp.

Pangaea's book of March

We have no passions left to love the spring / Who had suffered autumn as we did, alone
— Audre Lorde, "Second Spring"

in the March sky
I have written how to do

it, every year burning myself
through and swallowing oceans-full

of water, then crying it out into
the tiny veins of leaves, etc.

the winged mayfly, if born unlucky,
might think the world a sempiternal storm

but it takes years for a human to grow
wings, and reading the daily sky

you turn into yourself a little more
while the wings bloom out thinly

as blown glass, carry you into the
unseen river of things, no hands.

a star could pierce you now and
you'd only thank and become it

burning for a time, then
lighter.

the way faith cycles back around
spring sounds good to you now.

March sky
is a love letter, is

the parachute
stretched around horizon,

the paper
tethered to your spine.

ghazal for twins

after Aracelis Girmay

one brother unfolded from the other
where his father's hand was missing.

one mother was opened and drained
until her blood ran clear with fish.

owls flew from the operating table
dropping white paper wishes,

the twins called out, two constellations,
stars overflowing from their flesh.

a grass sky turned to fluorescent light
and her open mouth, her hundred stitches

could not stop the dawn in flight;
it came with fingers glistening.

bright and born, they rocked our eyes.
who would have known to listen?

they sang their every mirrored bone;
each was the other's christening.

the tiny gods they are have not yet
learned to flinch. to their perfect fists

and the lambent world they wield
we add nothing but our witness.

iv. when did you get so?

(alternate ending

a metaphor walks into a bar.

no, that's not what I meant,
that's what I said.

we trip toward the future
where we will all be covered
in hideous meanings and
will walk down the runway
with it
so stylish

we will all be gods and
will eat only brain foods
and will exfoliate with
quinoa plucked from
the sides of flying fish
that flew into the mountains
and stayed there.

we cannot wait to do
experiments on each other.
we cannot wait to turn
our next-door neighbor
into a robot at the church potluck.

we will spit Genesis like
rap automatons:
in the beginning
in the beginning
in the –
in the –
[scratching]
[the vinyl turning too fast
and melting at this point]

how many Jesuses does it take
to make a week?

is the question we will put
on every standardized test.
we will scratch and sniff
the bubble with number 2
razor blades
sharp as the teeth of our
favorite god,
and he will laugh like
something we buried
long before we had
enough words for the reek
of it, something we no longer
know how to explain.)

the other side

things here are not exactly
                    weightless
but they weigh less.
there is no money here.
there is an orphanage where
all the unrequited loves are
well taken care of.
          so you needn't worry.
a happy bunch, and on holidays
they make colorful jewelry.

you can see a Darling Downs
hopping mouse having tea
with a Caribbean monk seal
both fat and carefree.
here the ozone is a band
of cotton candy swaddling
the earth. it shines at night.

here there is
                    and there is not
not exactly more
but not less
just what was lost

here there are stations on
the side of the road where
you can cry on someone's
endless shoulder. you can
pinch a smell between your
fingers and tuck it into your
pocket. there is no use
for memory because here
everything is all at once.

here the non-mountains lay
uncrumpled and the tiny
asteroids that dot the There

still circle aimlessly in space.
here are car accidents in
reverse. here every trauma
pedals backward,
each body losing mass
as it spins and spins away.
here there is no need
for bodies.
            here consciousness
is a force and everyone holds
it by its front paws.

here the unpaired socks
and gloves from There
are used as flags
outside the little houses
and they mean nothing.

when a volcano erupts here
it's blood, not lava, that pours.
the rivers in Cuidad Juarez
and the DRC and the sides of
roads in the Middle East
dripped through the earth
and crossed over,
and here it's blood that
makes plants grow.

here there is no waste
            and it's just that
that
            which was place-
less There
is on the periodic table
here.

here there is no metal
not like There.
and here no one pretends

there are endings
and here you might as
well be blind because
seeing is nothing.
here all pain
converts to song
so you can't go anywhere
without music filling up
                the air.
here you might not
have a name

but that is okay because
your existence is the
most certain thing.

Pangaea's response to the Astronomy Department's recent announcement that it has discovered earth-eating stars[3]

life is
a gyrating flight from terravores.
you carbon preciousness.

this mothering is luck and labor
before voracious stars,
suns fattening with iron and blood,

a universe full of giants who could
eat your everything. hydrogen
dragons breathe a blaze

that has nothing to do with you.
in the light they belch are
the metal bones of other planets,

the specters of unlucky earths.
but this is not news, for you
are a planet of sun-worshipers,

sweaty skins and hands who know
to pray toward what could and does
not eat you.

prelude

the moon slick and O as a singing mouth
we could have eaten the   trumpeting frogs
we could have gotten wilder   popped the lake orches-
tra   into our mouths, each   musician coated with
       pollen sauce. the ticks   could have got-
ten wilder

strong-armed into the   Volkswagen and plunged

headfirst in the valley
       of our skin reaching up
       to suck clouds. I wanted to
sing,
       when did you get so?

       when you got so wild
       the poplars ahh-ed

       and the moon

with her aria held the long   C   and the
tire-

crushed onions
floated through the
       sunroof   you knocked

on every door
of my ghost town   the log cabins   disemboweled by ter-
mites
       the lullabies drowned   in glasses of water beside
       dust-packed mattresses.

       and you
brought me home outside.

over here, the stars
in my lungs were saying.

I've overgrown   through the years: my skin is purple in this light
my eyes are marble.

I've oxidized and become
brittle. but *over here* still

and with more wild

to sing   yet.

Notes

[1] Title based on the piece, "Tres mudances són pitjors que un incendi (Three Moves Are as Bad as a Fire)" (2013), a collection of photographic glass plates and accompanying field notes produced by the Lowell Expedition to the Andes during June and July 1907. On display at museum at Montjuïc, Barcelona, Spain.
[2] Title taken from the title of a book on display at the Museo del Libro Antiguo in Antigua, Guatemala.
[3] Salisbury, D. "Astronomers identify signature of Earth-eating stars." Research News @ Vanderbilt. 16 May 2014.

Acknowledgements

I am grateful to the journals and organizations that first published or honored several of the poems:
"Primum non nocere" The Los Angeles Review
"the benediction of Our Lady of Hyperglycemia" the museum of americana
"what's your name" Love Insha'Allah blog
"nuestra Señora de Tennessee supplicates Coatlalopeuh," "thermodynamics," and "hydronymy" HEArt Journal
"Prelude" Callaloo Journal
"Pangaea's 16 questions" and "(alternate ending" Jet Fuel Review
"glossopteris" Lime Hawk Arts
"g as in god" The Scream" (online anthology about dreams)
"observation in a small country" and "the law of conservation of love" Big Lucks

"The weight and dimensions of my prayers" and "the Black American gets her travel fellowship and goes abroad" won Honorable Mention and Editor's Choice, respectively, in the Sandy Crimmins National Poetry contest. These poems were published in Philadelphia Stories. "theory of multiple theories" was a finalist for the 2016 Brittany Noakes Poetry Award.

Thanks to the 2014 Callaloo workshop, in particular to Vievee Francis and Gregory Pardlo, for pushing me to deepen my poetry at a time that was critical for the creation of this book.

A special thanks to my Callaloo colleague and friend Kimberly Reyes, whose thoughtful reading and honest insights were indispensable to several of these poems.

Thanks to the Tennessee Valley Agrarian Poets' Society, a group of doctor-poets at Vanderbilt University, with whom I worked on many of these poems. Their dissections of my poetry were vital exercises.

Thanks to my mentor Dr. Shari Barkin, for understanding what it means to be a physician-artist and for supporting me in the dual pursuit.

I have much appreciation for dancing girl press & studio for publishing my chapbook in 2014 and inspiring me to imagine the book you hold in your hands today. Thanks to Megan Kaminski for seeing this manuscript, and to Trembling Pillow Press for turning my vision into a reality.

To Rashmi Joshi, Mohammad Torabinejad, Maura Mathieu, Shayma Jannat, and Sherif Abdelkarim, some of my earliest readers, thanks for holding me accountable to my words.

Thank you to Justin Reid, a muse who never tires of listening to my poetry and poetic ideas.

Thank you to my grandparents, whose stories of New Orleans inspire my re-imagining of our family's home place and my place in the world.

To my siblings, Jeannette and Benoît, who invented all manner of things with me in our TV-less childhood – new religions, countries in our backyard, social justice organizations, time travel, et cetera – you two nourished my imagination from the very beginning.

Finally, thanks to my parents, Cathie and Michael. My mother was my scribe when I was two and not yet able to write although I wanted to; my father was the dream-keeper who made sure I never stopped writing. Without them this book would not exist.

Irène Mathieu is a pediatrician, writer, and public health researcher who has lived and worked in the United States, the Dominican Republic, Guatemala, Peru, and elsewhere. She has been a Pushcart Prize nominee, a Callaloo fellow, and a Fulbright scholar. Irène is the author of the poetry chapbook *the galaxy of origins* (dancing girl press, 2014). She holds a BA in International Relations from the College of William & Mary and a MD from Vanderbilt University.

Trembling Pillow Press

I of the Storm by Bill Lavender

Olympia Street by Michael Ford

Ethereal Avalanche by Gina Ferrara

Transfixion by Bill Lavender

Downtown by Lee Meitzen Grue

SONG OF PRAISE   Homage To John Coltrane by John Sinclair

DESERT JOURNAL by ruth weiss

Aesthesia Balderdash by Kim Vodicka

SUPER NATURAL by Tracey McTague

I LOVE THIS AMERICAN WAY OF LIFE by Brett Evans

Q by Bill Lavender

loaded arc by Laura Goldstein

Want for Lion by Paige Taggart

Trick Rider by Jen Tynes

May Apple Deep by Michael Sikkema

Gossamer Lid by Andrew Brezna

simple constructs for the lizzies by Lisa Cattrone

FILL: A Collection by Kate Schapira and Erika Howsare

Red of Split Water a burial rite by Lisa Donovan

Forthcoming Titles:
CUNTRY by Kristin Sanders
Kids of the Black Hole by Marty Cain
If You Love Error So Love Zero by Stephanie Anderson
Feelings by Lauren Ireland

Trembling Pillow Press

Bob Kaufman Book Prize

2012: *Of Love & Capital* by Christopher Rizzo (Bernadette Mayer, judge)

2013: *Psalms for Dogs and Sorcerers* by Jen Coleman (Dara Wier, judge)

2014: *Natural Subjets* by Divya Victor (Anselm Berrigan, judge)

2015: *there are boxes and there is wanting* by Tessa Micaela Landreau-Grasmuck (Laura Mullen, judge)

2016 *orogeny* by Irène Mathieu (Megan Kaminski, judge)

Praise for *orogeny:*

Orogeny buries deep into rock and soil, silence and speech, into the pulse of what connects us as mothers, sisters, lovers, and ghosts—the quest for home and for a language that can account for both what might become and what has been lost. Searching ecologies, history, and embodied experience, Irène Mathieu's lyric voice pieces together a world, which is at once our own and a map of possibility, a "fetal dream of ourselves, a sea of curled and floating ideas."
    —Megan Kaminski, author of *Deep City,* judge of the 2016 Bob Kaufman Book Prize

In *orogeny*, wisewoman and mythkeeper Irène Mathieu fiercely erects a "pharmacy of noises," a mountain of love poems to what it means to be precariously human, an awakening fist armed with the might of dreams against the things that plague the earth and us: murder, hate, wars, borders. This collection is a hymn for the puzzling anatomy of survival, the evolution of rage, and the healing prism of wanderlust. These poems serve as "proper rites" against the violence of language that accompanies what has become the world's textbook physical ruthlessness. Mathieu penetrates the dust and fragments of our earthly existence—all that's been lost and left behind—and sings it back together. I could "drink these poems" with their old eyes for an eternity, and they would be enuf, all I need.
    —Yolanda Wisher, author of *Monk Eats an Afro,* Poet Laureate of Philadelphia 2016-17

It's apt that one of the central images of orogeny is that of Pangaea because Irène Mathieu broke me, over & over & over & infinite. *Orogeny* takes its reader across many different histories—of family, of continents, of violences, of sciences, of dirts, of fears, of soils, of loves—and every one is bigger than the last. It asks its reader, "what do I deserve?" and while the reader stares at it in amazement it answers "everything inside the moon." In an existence as fractured as this one, orogeny is not just the myth that we need; it's the then (& now & future) that we deserve.
    —Mark Cugini, author of *I'm Just Happy to Be Here*, managing books editor, *Big Lucks Books*

Made in the USA
Middletown, DE
16 April 2019